May I Please?

by Kyla Steinkraus

Content Consultants:
Melissa Z. Pierce, L.C.S.W.
Sam Williams, M.Ed.

Rourke
Educational Media
rourkeeducationalmedia.com

Teacher Notes available at
rem4teachers.com

www.rourkeeducationalmedia.com

Melissa Z. Pierce is a licensed clinical social worker with a background in counseling in the home and school group settings. Melissa is currently a life coach. She brings her experience as a L.C.S.W. and parent to the *Little World Social Skills* collection and the *Social Skills and More* program.

Sam Williams has a master's degree in education. Sam is a former teacher with over ten years of classroom experience. He has been a literacy coach, professional development writer and trainer, and is a published author. He brings his experience in child development and classroom management to this series.

PHOTO CREDITS: Cover: © Sean Locke; page 3: © Sean Locke; page 5: © Sharon Meredith; page 7: © Rosemarie Gearhart; page 9: © David Hernandez; page 11: © Dmitry Lastovich; page 12: © Robert Churchill; page 13: © Agnieszka Kirinicjanow; page 15: © Agnieszka Kirinicjanow; page 17: © Gregory Johnston; page 18: © Christopher Futcher; page 19: © Cliff Parnell; page 20: © kali9; page 21: © Yuko Hirao

Illustrations by: Anita DuFalla

Edited by: Precious McKenzie

Cover and Interior designed by: Tara Raymo

Library of Congress PCN Data

May I Please? / Kyla Steinkraus
(Little World Social Skills)
ISBN 978-1-61810-138-9 (hard cover)(alk. paper)
ISBN 978-1-61810-271-3 (soft cover)
Library of Congress Control Number: 2011945283

Rourke Educational Media
Printed in the United States of America,
North Mankato, Minnesota

rourkeeducationalmedia.com

customerservice@rourkeeducationalmedia.com • PO Box 643328 Vero Beach, Florida 32964

What are **manners**? Words like "please" and "thank you" show **kindness**.

Having good manners means you are **polite**.

You use good manners when you help someone. You can be helpful by opening a door for someone or offering to set the dinner table.

Practicing good manners helps us be good **friends** to one another. It shows we care about other people.

Follow the Golden Rule: Treat people the way you want to be treated.

At the dinner table say, "May I please have some more food?"

Say "please" and "thank you" all the time, even when you think no one else is using their manners.

You can share toys with your friends.
When you want a **turn**, you say,
"May I please take a turn?"

Taking turns while playing a video game lets everyone enjoy the fun.

What would you say if you want to borrow a toy from a friend?

That's right! "May I please?"

What do you say when you ask to speak with someone on the telephone?

That's right! "May I please?"

Can you think of other times you would need your best manners?

When you act in a kind and **thoughtful** way towards other people, they want to be friends with you!

Everyone enjoys spending time with a person who is polite, so please practice being polite.

Practice It!

Pretend you are at a restaurant.

How should you ask to be seated?

How should you order your food?

What do you say to the server when it is time to leave?

Picture Glossary

friends (frendz):
People you know and like and who like you too.

kindness (KINDE-nis):
To be helpful and friendly.

manners (MAN-urs):
Acting polite and kind.

polite (puh-LITE):
To be thoughtful and considerate of others.

thoughtful (THAWT-fuhl):
Giving careful attention to the needs of others.

turn (turn): When two or more people share the use of something.

Index

Websites

pbskids.org/barney/children/storytime/please1.html

www.nea.org/tools/lessons/learning-and-practicing-
  good-manners-grades-K-5.html

www.preschooleducation.com/smanners.shtml

About the Author

Kyla Steinkraus lives in Tampa, Florida, with her husband and two children. She and her five-year-old son remind each other to say 'please' when one of them forgets (which isn't very often).

Ask The Author!
www.rem4students.com